Atoms and Molecules

by Tracy Nelson Maurer

Science Content Editor:
Shirley Duke

Educational Media

rourkeeducationalmedia.com

Teacher Notes available at
rem4teachers.com

Science Content Editor: Shirley Duke holds a bachelor's degree in biology and a master's degree in education from Austin College in Sherman, Texas. She taught science in Texas at all levels for twenty-five years before starting to write for children. Her science books include *You Can't Wear These Genes, Infections, Infestations, and Diseases, Enterprise STEM, Forces and Motion at Work, Environmental Disasters,* and *Gases.* She continues writing science books and also works as a science content editor.

www.rourkeeducationalmedia.com

The author thanks materials science engineer Michael Sullivan for his generous assistance.

Photo credits: Cover © Jut; Pages 2/3 © Viktor88; Pages 4/5 © Stuart Monk, Vladru; Pages 6/7 © Blue Door Publishing; Pages 8/9 courtesy of The Library of Congress, © MrJafari, ELECTRON CLOUD IMAGE; Pages 10/11 © concept w, Mike Price; Pages 12/13 © concept w, Jurii; Pages 14/15 © concept w, Christian Lopetz; Pages 16/17 © Zhabska Tetyana, Ikunl, Viktor88; Pages 18/19 © glossyplastic, Paul Hakimata Photography; Pages 20/21 © Michael Schmid, Christian Darkin

Editor: Kelli Hicks

My Science Library series produced by Blue Door Publishing, Florida for Rourke Educational Media.

Library of Congress PCN Data

Maurer, Tracy Nelson.
 Atoms and Molecules / Tracy Nelson Maurer.
    p. cm. -- (My Science Library)
 ISBN 978-1-61810-106-8(Hard cover) (alk. paper)
 ISBN 978-1-61810-239-3 (Soft cover)
 Library of Congress Control Number: 2012930304

Rourke Educational Media
Printed in the United States of America,
North Mankato, Minnesota

rourkeeducationalmedia.com

customerservice@rourkeeducationalmedia.com   •   PO Box 643328 Vero Beach, Florida 32964

Table of Contents

Tiny Ingredients

The ancient Greek philosopher Democritus believed if you continued cutting a material by halves, you would find a particle that could not be divided. He called it the atom, a word that means indivisible.

In the early 1800s, the English scientist John Dalton revived the idea of atoms in his studies of gases. His work led to our modern atomic theory.

John Dalton (1766–1844) first earned recognition in 1794 for his research on color blindness, a condition he had. Later, he developed a model of atoms and theories of their behaviors based on careful scientific measurement.

John Dalton

atom

Everything around us, both natural and man-made, is made up of atoms.

Protons, Neutrons, and Electrons

●○●○●○●○●○●○●○●○●○●○●○●

Inside each atom, small particles give it the power to build materials.

A clump of protons and neutrons form the nucleus at the center of the atom. Protons hold a positive electrical charge. Neutrons have no charge.

Small electrons swarm at high speeds around the nucleus. They carry a negative charge that balances the positively charged protons.

Atomic Fact

An atom normally has the same number of electrons as protons.

The Structure of An Atom

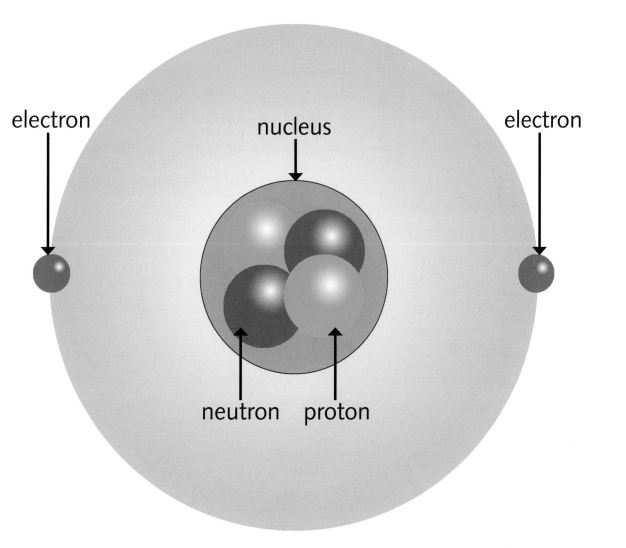

electron

nucleus

electron

neutron   proton

Atomic Fact

Atoms are so small they can't be seen. They are studied by how they behave. Protons and neutrons are about the same mass, but electrons are much smaller. Imagine a tennis ball as a nucleus and pinheads as electrons. A model formed on this scale would be about 2,300 feet (700 meters) in diameter!

Ernest Rutherford

Ernest Rutherford (1871–1937) studied radioactive materials, especially the rays coming from some materials. He discovered that atoms have nuclei and went on to work with others to show how radioactive atoms break down.

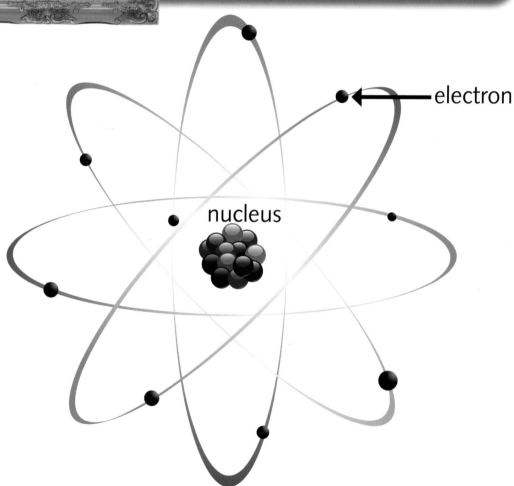

electron

nucleus

An atom's particles move all the time. Electrons and their motion energy keep them from crashing into the nucleus and help hold the atom together.

Electrons don't follow an exact **orbit**. The electrons flow in layers, called shells. They form a cloud around the nucleus.

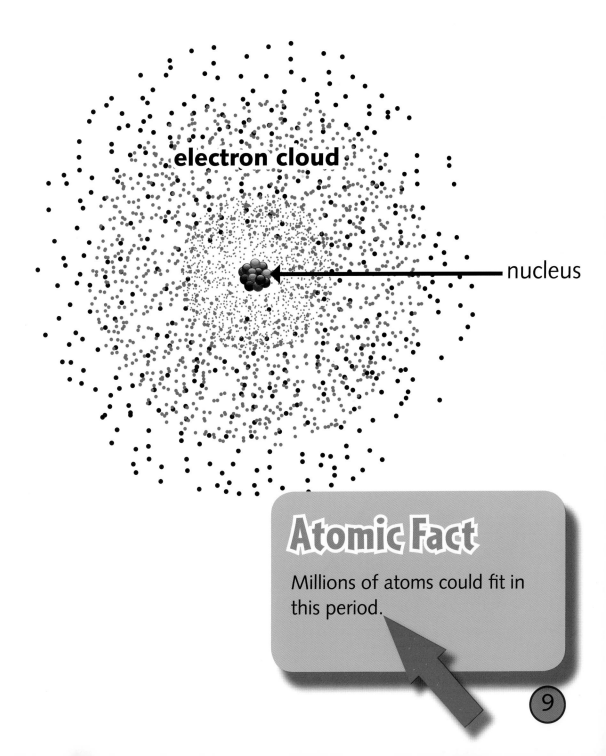

electron cloud

nucleus

Atomic Fact

Millions of atoms could fit in this period.

The Elements

● ● ● ● ● ● ● ● ● ● ● ● ● ●

Elements are the basic ingredients for everything in the universe.

Each element is made of like atoms. All of them have the same number of protons. That number of protons equals the element's unique **atomic number**.

For example, hydrogen gas atoms with one proton have an atomic number of one. Only hydrogen atoms together act like the gas it is, meaning it has the same **properties**. In combination with different atoms, the properties are different.

atomic number

Atomic Fact

So far, scientists have found 118 elements. Ninety-four elements occur naturally. Scientists created the others.

Hydrogen

Helium

Lithium

Beryllium

Boron

Carbon

Nitrogen

Oxygen

Fluorine

Neon

Neutron

Proton

Electron

Period 1 and 2 Elements

In 1869, Russian scientist Dmitri Mendeleev developed the periodic table. He listed the elements in rows, from the smallest to largest known **atomic weight**.

He started a new row when properties began to repeat. He found that similar properties occurred at regular intervals, or periods.

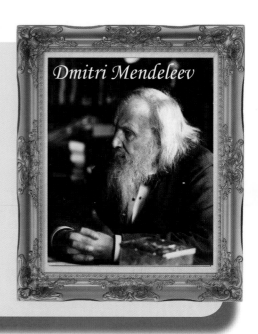

Dmitri Mendeleev

Dmitri Mendeleev organized the elements by their atomic weight, or approximate number of protons and neutrons for each atom, in 1869. Back then, just 62 elements were known.

Other scientists created tables, too, but only Mendeleev's table anticipated yet undiscovered elements based on their properties. **Germanium**, discovered in 1886, showed Mendeleev's table worked.

Germanium is a chemical element with the symbol Ge and atomic number 32. Germanium is found in ores and most of it comes from smelting zinc ores. It is used in semiconductors, alloys, optical equipment, electric guitar amps, and in camera and microscope lenses.

Atomic Fact

The periodic table still changes. In 2010, scientists officially named copernicium (Cn, atomic number 112). In 2011, scientists accepted ununquadium (Uuq, atomic number 114) and ununhexium (Uuh, atomic number 116).

Today's Periodic Table

Just as Mendeleev's did, today's periodic table uses letters for the element names, such as O for oxygen.

Elements stand in columns, aligned by their properties. For example, the gap between hydrogen (H) and helium (He) puts helium in the column with gases that do not normally **bond** with other elements.

Today's table, however, also lists the elements in rows by atomic number. Atomic numbers weren't understood until the early 1900s.

Period	Group 1	2	3	4	5
1	1 **H** 1.008				
2	3 **Li** 6.941	4 **Be** 9.012			
3	11 **Na** 22.99	12 **Mg** 24.31			
4	19 **K** 39.10	20 **Ca** 40.08	21 **Sc** 44.96	22 **Ti** 47.88	23 **V** 50.9
5	37 **Rb** 85.47	38 **Sr** 87.62	39 **Y** 88.91	40 **Zr** 91.22	41 **N** 92.1
6	55 **Cs** 132.9	56 **Ba** 137.3	*	72 **Hf** 178.5	73 **Ta** 180
7	87 **Fr** (223)	88 **Ra** (226)	**	104 **Rf** (261)	105 **D** (26

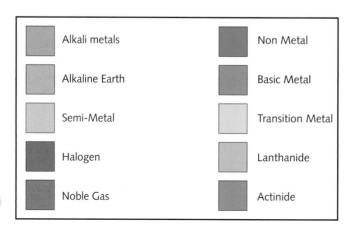

Alkali metals		Non Metal	
Alkaline Earth		Basic Metal	
Semi-Metal		Transition Metal	
Halogen		Lanthanide	
Noble Gas		Actinide	

*Lanthanide Series

**Actinide Series

57 **La** 138.9	58 **C** 140
89 **Ac** (227)	90 **T** 23

Element: Carbon

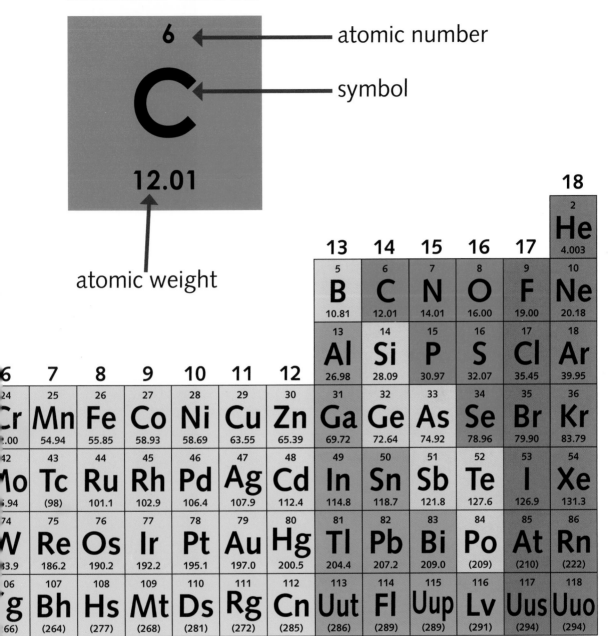

6 ← atomic number

C ← symbol

12.01

atomic weight

18
2 **He** 4.003

13	14	15	16	17
5 **B** 10.81	6 **C** 12.01	7 **N** 14.01	8 **O** 16.00	9 **F** 19.00	10 **Ne** 20.18
13 **Al** 26.98	14 **Si** 28.09	15 **P** 30.97	16 **S** 32.07	17 **Cl** 35.45	18 **Ar** 39.95

6	7	8	9	10	11	12
24 **Cr** .00	25 **Mn** 54.94	26 **Fe** 55.85	27 **Co** 58.93	28 **Ni** 58.69	29 **Cu** 63.55	30 **Zn** 65.39	31 **Ga** 69.72	32 **Ge** 72.64	33 **As** 74.92	34 **Se** 78.96	35 **Br** 79.90	36 **Kr** 83.79
42 **Mo** 5.94	43 **Tc** (98)	44 **Ru** 101.1	45 **Rh** 102.9	46 **Pd** 106.4	47 **Ag** 107.9	48 **Cd** 112.4	49 **In** 114.8	50 **Sn** 118.7	51 **Sb** 121.8	52 **Te** 127.6	53 **I** 126.9	54 **Xe** 131.3
74 **W** 3.9	75 **Re** 186.2	76 **Os** 190.2	77 **Ir** 192.2	78 **Pt** 195.1	79 **Au** 197.0	80 **Hg** 200.5	81 **Tl** 204.4	82 **Pb** 207.2	83 **Bi** 209.0	84 **Po** (209)	85 **At** (210)	86 **Rn** (222)
06 **g** 66)	107 **Bh** (264)	108 **Hs** (277)	109 **Mt** (268)	110 **Ds** (281)	111 **Rg** (272)	112 **Cn** (285)	113 **Uut** (286)	114 **Fl** (289)	115 **Uup** (289)	116 **Lv** (291)	117 **Uus** (294)	118 **Uuo** (294)

59 **Pr** 40.9	60 **Nd** 144.2	61 **Pm** (145)	62 **Sm** 150.4	63 **Eu** 152.0	64 **Gd** 157.2	65 **Tb** 158.9	66 **Dy** 162.5	67 **Ho** 164.9	68 **Er** 167.3	69 **Tm** 168.9	70 **Yb** 173.0	71 **Lu** 175.0
91 **Pa** 31	92 **U** 238	93 **Np** (237)	94 **Pu** (244)	95 **Am** (243)	96 **Cm** (247)	97 **Bk** (247)	98 **Cf** (251)	99 **Es** (252)	100 **Fm** (257)	101 **Md** (258)	102 **No** (259)	103 **Lr** (262)

Molecules and Compounds

●○○○○○○○○○○○○○○○○○○

Molecules form when two or more atoms bond. These atoms can be from the same element or from different elements.

For example, two atoms of oxygen together make the oxygen molecule that's in the air we breathe.

oxygen molecule

oxygen atom   oxygen atom

When two or more atoms from elements bond, they form a **compound**. The tiniest particle of a compound is a molecule. Two hydrogen atoms bonded with one oxygen atom create a water molecule. Water is a common compound.

water molecule

oxygen atom

hydrogen atom

hydrogen atom

Water is life's most important compound molecule. Without water, no living creature can survive.

To bond in compounds, atoms may share electrons or send or receive electrons from each other. Some compounds happen naturally, such as water molecules.

People manufacture many other compounds. They create **chemical reactions** that either add or break apart molecules to produce everything from nylon fishing lines to deadly weapons.

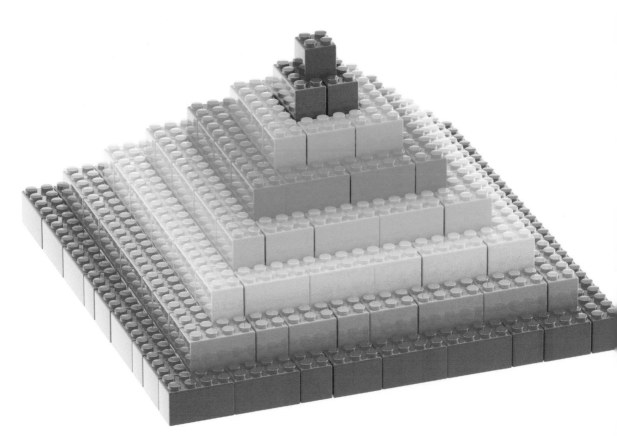

The elements hydrogen and carbon combine to form hydrocarbons. Hydrocarbon molecules rearranged into very long chains make plastics, such as these toys.

Atomic Fact

Carbon forms more compounds than any other element except hydrogen. Some carbon compounds include:
- Vitamins
- Sugar
- Gasoline
- Plastic
- All living things—yes, you!

Many man-made compounds are based on compounds that occur in nature. For example, instead of using carrots to dye clothing orange, scientists invented man-made dyes that last longer and look brighter.

What More Can Atoms Do?

More than two thousand years after Democritus discussed atoms, the scanning tunneling microscope (STM) finally allowed scientists to see images of atomic structures.

Atomic Fact

The STM shoots an electrical charge to the tip of a probe hovering extremely close to a surface. Electrons tunnel across the tiny gap. A computer measures the tunneling to create a dimensional image.

Surfaces that look flat to the naked eye have dimensional shapes when seen with an STM.

copper surface

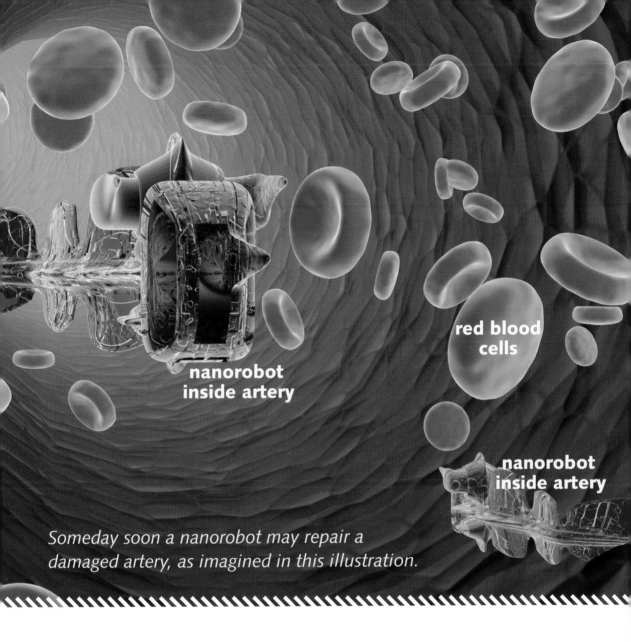

red blood cells

nanorobot inside artery

nanorobot inside artery

Someday soon a nanorobot may repair a damaged artery, as imagined in this illustration.

STM technology has helped to open a new field of atomic study called **nanoscience**. Researchers have already tapped nanoscience to develop cancer treatments, computer data systems, water filters, and other products. In time, the tiniest particles may unlock the world's biggest mysteries.

Show What You Know

1. What is the basic arrangement of the parts of an atom?

2. Can you think of other natural molecules besides water?

3. If you could build an atomic beam that was good for humans, what would it *do*? How would it work?

Glossary

atomic number (uh-TAH-mik NUHM-bur): the number of protons in the nucleus of the atoms for each element

atomic weight (uh-TAH-mik WATE): the average mass of the different forms of atoms in each element

bond (BOND): the connection that joins two atoms or molecules to create a material

chemical reactions (KEM-i-kuhl ree-AK-shuhnz): processes that add to molecules or break apart molecules to create new substances

compound (KAHM-pound): matter formed of two or more molecules

germanium (juhr-MAY-nee-uhm): the element (Ge) with an atomic number of 32 that is a shiny, gray type of metal

molecules (MAH-luh-kyoolz): the smallest bit of a substance that retains all the characteristics of the substance; a combination of like or different atoms

nanoscience (NAN-oh-SYE-uhns): the study of things measured in billionths of a meter, especially individual molecules

orbit (OR-bit): a path that travels around and around something

properties (PRAH-pur-teez): qualities or traits of something

Index

Websites to Visit

www.kidskonnect.com/subject-index/15-science/60-atoms.html

www.tpt.org/newtons/index.php

www.webelements.com/

About the Author

Tracy Nelson Maurer likes science experiments, especially the cooking kind! She lives in Minnesota with her husband and two children. She holds an MFA in Writing for Children and Young Adults from Hamline University.

Ask The Author!
www.rem4students.com